Famous & Fun Favorites
13 Appealing Piano Arrangements
Carol Matz

Nothing is more motivating for students than playing something familiar. *Famous & Fun Favorites, Book 5,* is a collection of 13 carefully selected familiar songs that students are sure to know and love. These intermediate arrangements can be used as a supplement to any method. Book 5 introduces sixteenth notes, and features arrangements in key signatures with up to two sharps or flats. Enjoy your musical experience with these time-tested favorites!

Carol Matz

Second Edition
Copyright © MMV by Alfred Publishing Co., Inc.
All rights reserved.   Printed in USA.
ISBN 0-7390-3775-7

Yankee Doodle Dandy

George M. Cohan
Arr. by Carol Matz

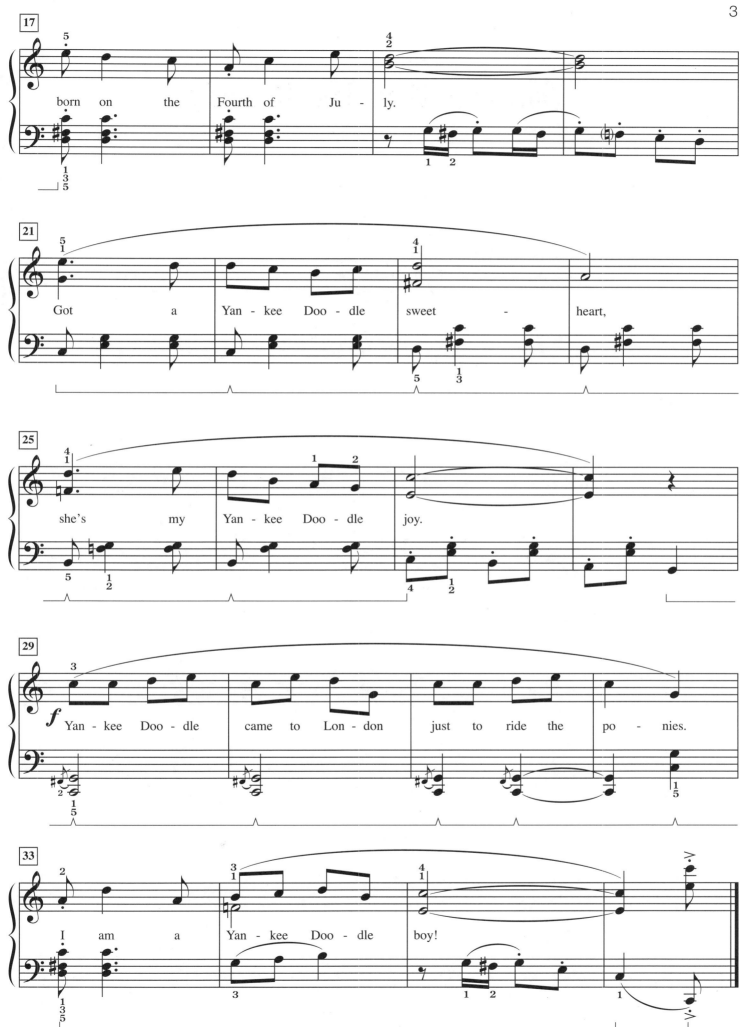

Mexican Hat Dance

Traditional
Arr. by Carol Matz

The Caissons Go Rolling Along

U.S. Army Song
Arr. by Carol Matz

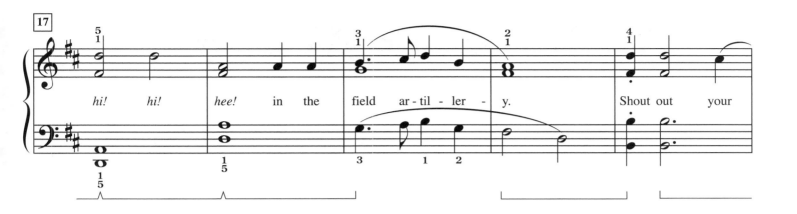

hi! hi! hee! in the field ar-til-ler - y. Shout out your

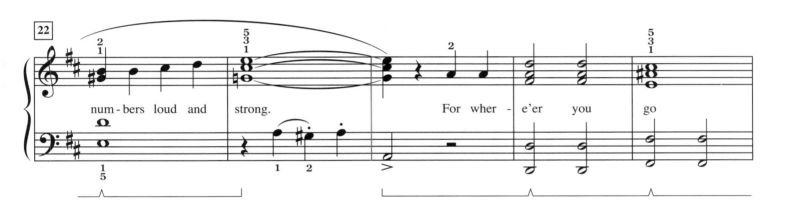

num-bers loud and strong. For wher - e'er you go

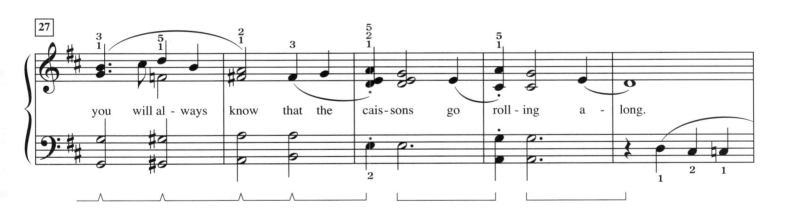

you will al - ways know that the cais-sons go roll-ing a - long.

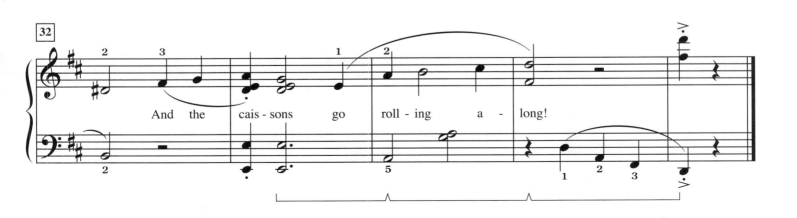

And the cais-sons go roll-ing a - long!

Carnival of Venice

Traditional Italian
Arr. by Carol Matz

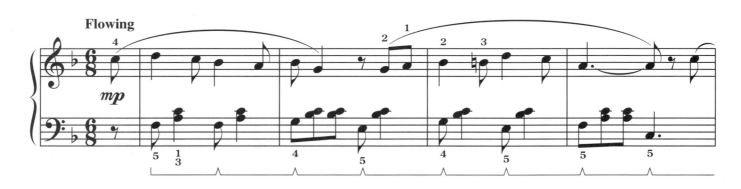

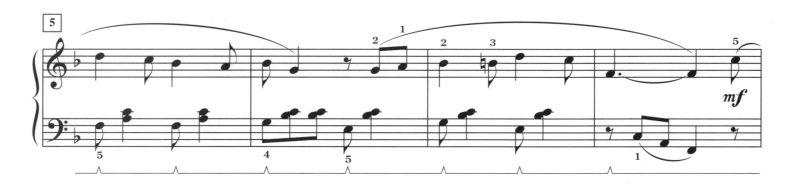

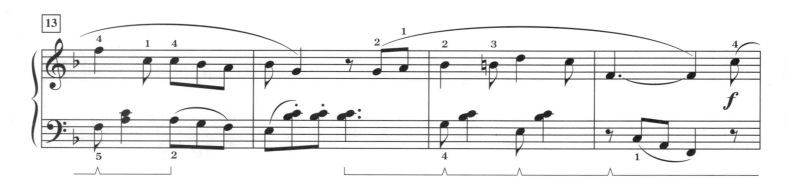

Scarborough Fair

Traditional English
Arr. by Carol Matz

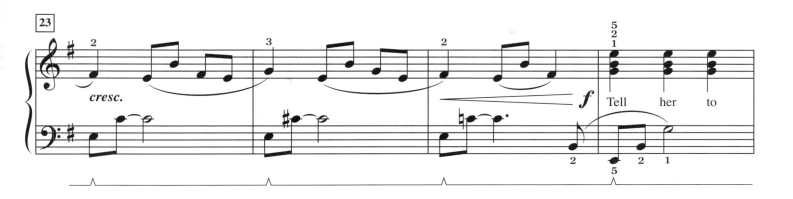

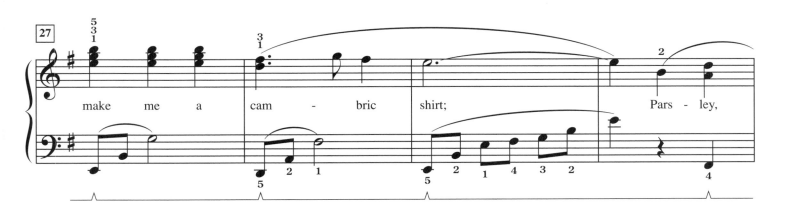

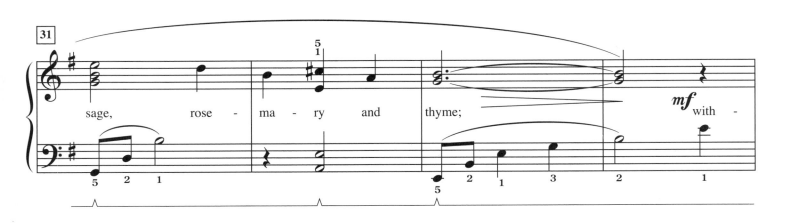

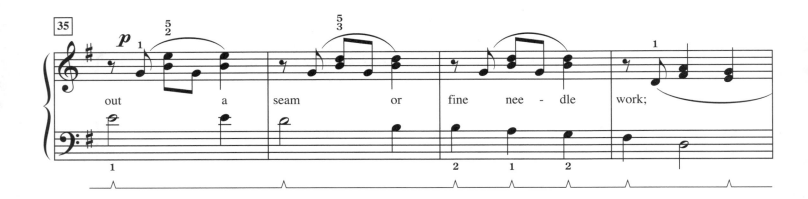

out   a   seam   or   fine   nee - dle   work;

then   she'll   be   a   true   love   of

mine.

Sailing, Sailing

Godfrey Marks
Arr. by Carol Matz

Alexander's Ragtime Band

Irving Berlin
Arr. by Carol Matz

Washington Post March

John Philip Sousa
Arr. by Carol Matz

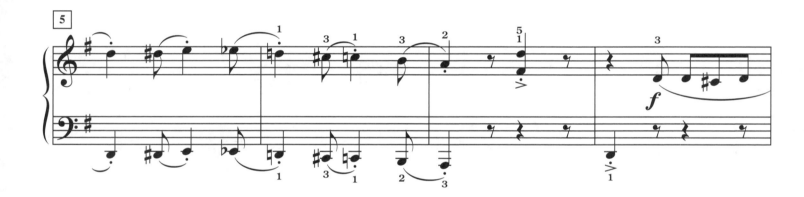

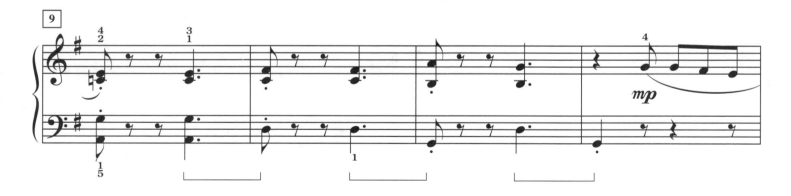

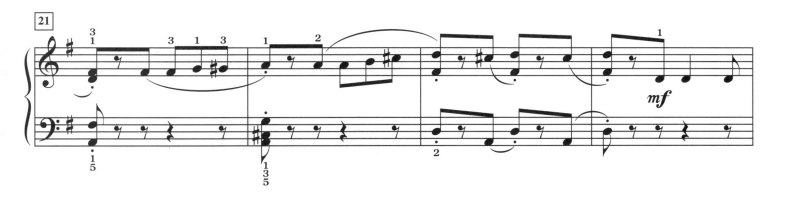

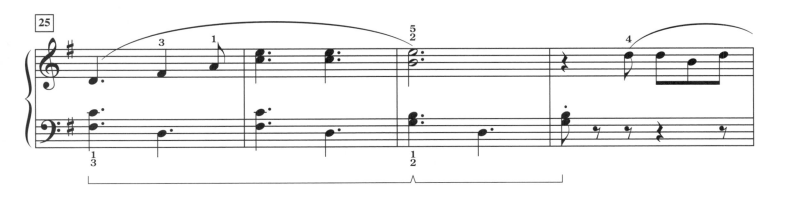

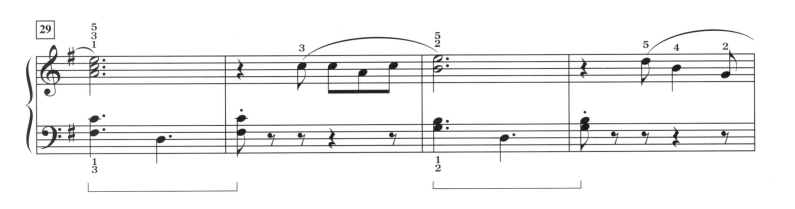

Down by the Riverside

Traditional Spiritual
Arr. by Carol Matz

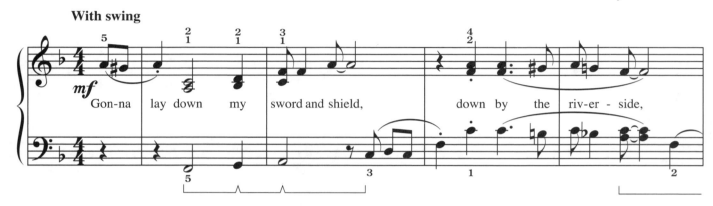

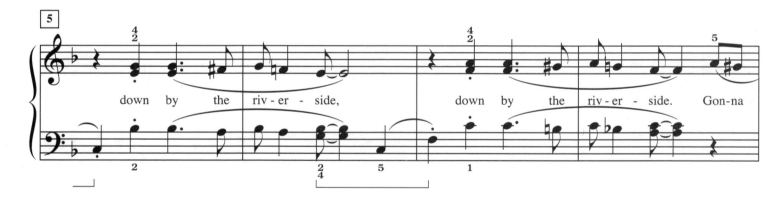

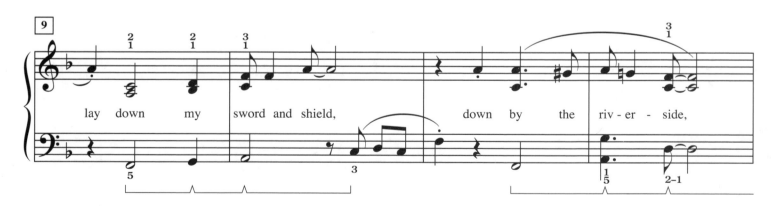

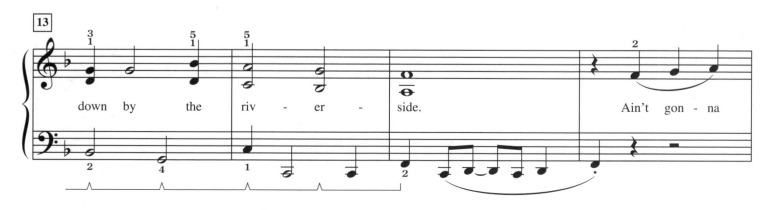

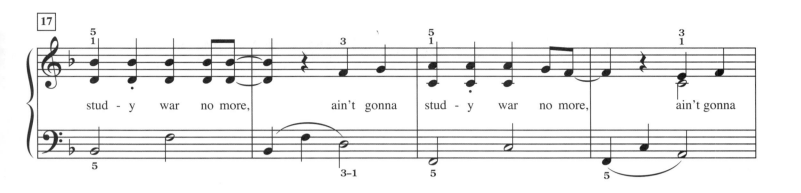

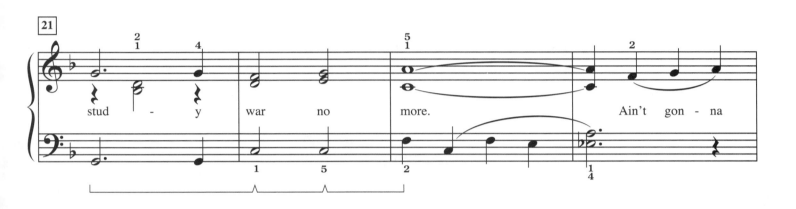

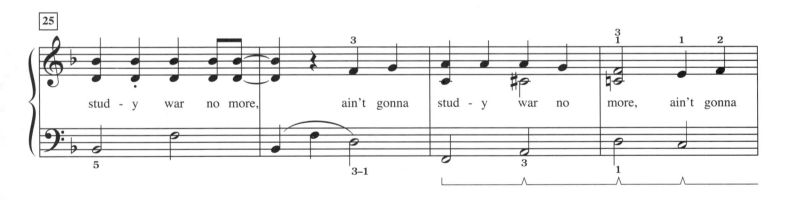

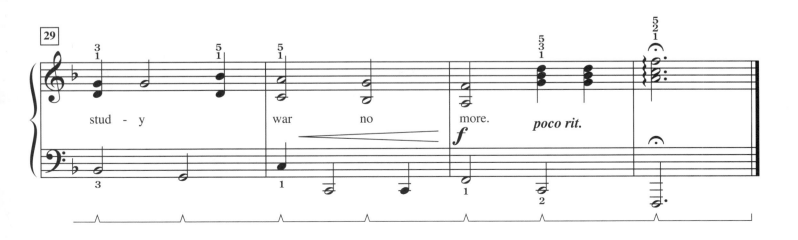

The Star-Spangled Banner

Words by Francis Scott Key
Music by John Stafford Smith
Arr. by Carol Matz

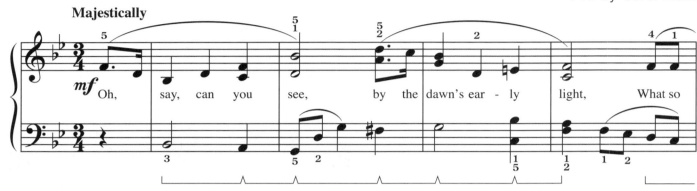

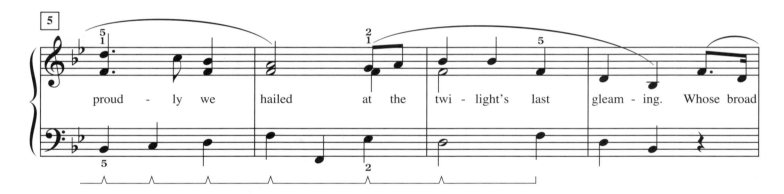

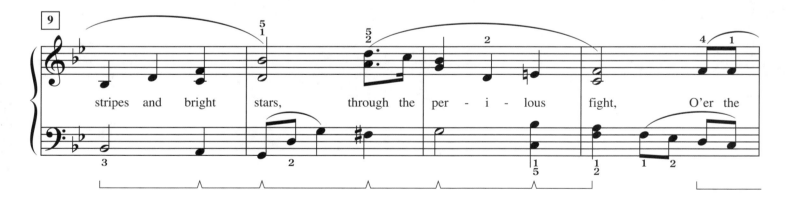

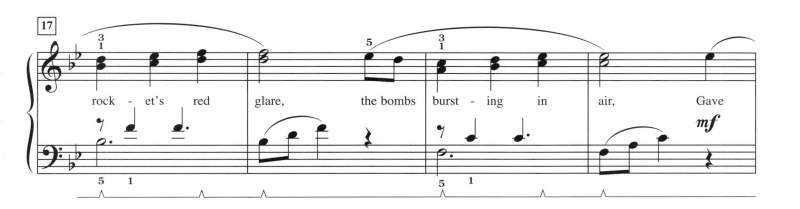

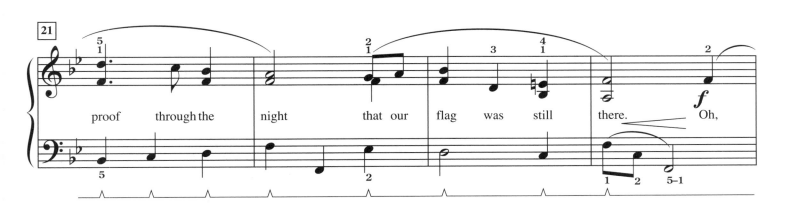

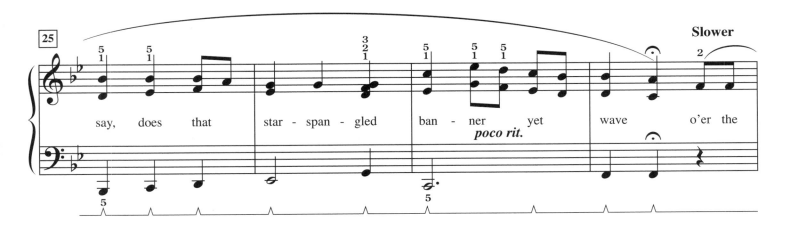

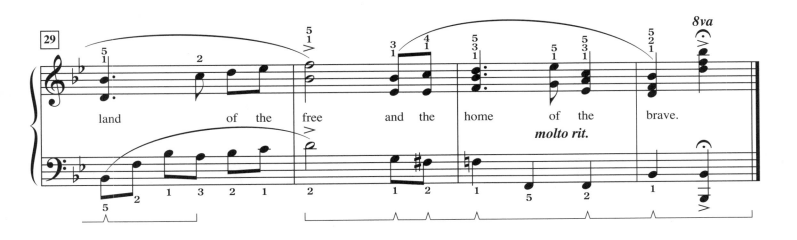

Maple Leaf Rag

Scott Joplin
Arr. by Carol Matz

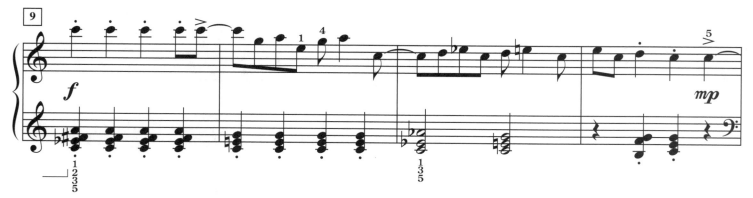

Hava Nagila

Israeli Folk Song
Arr. by Carol Matz

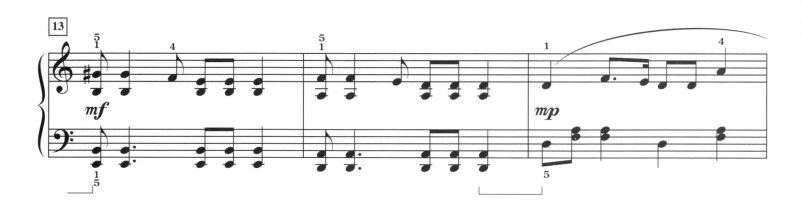

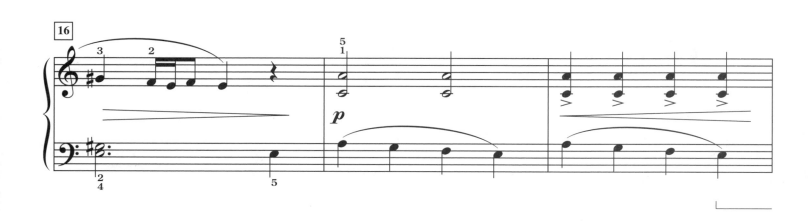

America

(My Country, 'Tis of Thee)

Traditional Melody
Words by Samuel F. Smith
Arr. by Carol Matz

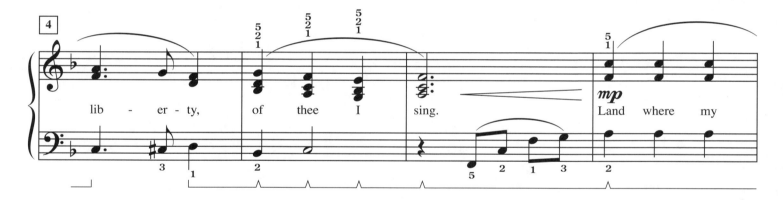

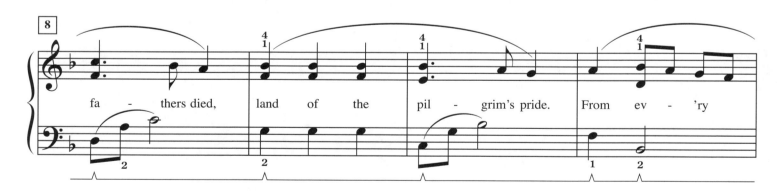

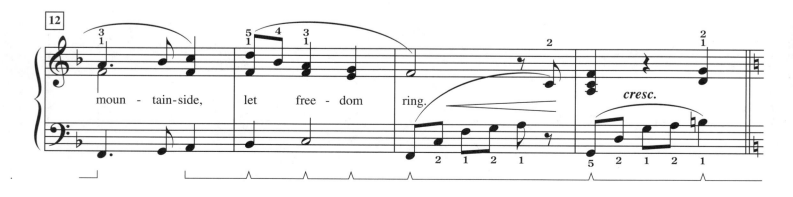

* Top notes of left-hand octaves are optional.

Famous & Fun series

Christmas • Classics • Favorites • Pop

Famous & Fun Favorites from the Famous & Fun series provides valuable supplementary material that has been carefully selected for student appeal. These effective and enjoyable arrangements can supplement any piano method and provide motivating recital material.

Highlights of the Famous & Fun series:
• carefully selected pieces
• well-graded arrangements
• levels remain consistent throughout the seri
• musical, motivating arrangements
• optional duet parts (Books 1–3)

Carol Matz is an active composer, arranger, author and editor of educational piano materials. She also maintains a piano studio where she enjoys teaching students of all ages and abilities.

Carol studied composition, arranging and orchestration at the University of Miami, with an emphasis on studio and jazz writing. In addition to her compositions and arrangements for piano, Carol has written for a variety of ensembles including orchestra, jazz big band and string quartet. Her work also includes studio arrangements and recording sessions for a number of artists in Miami-area recording studios. Carol serves as a keyboard editor for Alfred.

Famous & Fun Favorites, Book 1
(21392)
(Early Elementary)

Alouette
The Bear Went Over
  the Mountain
Camptown Races
Humpty Dumpty
Hush, Little Baby
Mary Had a Little Lamb
The Mulberry Bush
Row, Row, Row
  Your Boat
Shoo, Fly
This Old Man
Twinkle, Twinkle,
  Little Star
The Wheels on the Bus
Yankee Doodle

Famous & Fun Favorites, Book 2
(21393)
(Early Elementary to Elementary)

America the Beautiful
The Ants Go Marching
Auld Lang Syne
Bingo
Boom, Boom! (Ain't It
  Great to Be Crazy?)
Hickory, Dickory, Dock
John Jacob
  Jingleheimer Schmidt
La Cucaracha
Looby Loo
The Man on the
  Flying Trapeze
The Old Gray Mare
Over the River and
  Through the Woods
Pop! Goes the Weasel
Six Little Ducks
Take Me Out to the
  Ball Game
When the Saints Go
  Marching In

Famous & Fun Favorites, Book 3
(21394)
(Elementary to Late Elementary)

Baby Bumblebee
Down by the Bay
Home on the Range
I've Been Workin' on
  the Railroad
It Ain't Gonna Rain No More
The Mexican
  Clapping Song
Michael Finnegan
The Noble Duke of York
Oh, My Darling Clementine
Polly Wolly Doodle
Skip to My Lou
The Stars and
  Stripes Forever
The Yellow Rose of Texas
You're a Grand Old Flag

Famous & Fun Favorites, Book 4
(23250)
(Early Intermediate)

America the Beautiful
Battle Hymn of the Republic
The Entertainer
The Erie Canal
Funiculi, Funicula
Greensleeves
Irish Washerwoman
La Bamba
The Riddle Song
  (I Gave My Love a Cherry)
The Skaters Waltz
The Snake Charmer
Swing Low, Sweet Chariot
The Thunderer
Turkey in the Straw
Wedding Tarantella
You're a Grand Old Flag

Famous & Fun Favorites, Book 5
(23251)
(Intermediate)

Alexander's Ragtime Band
America (My Country, 'Tis of Thee)
The Caissons Go Rolling Along
Carnival of Venice
Down by the Riverside
Hava Nagila
Maple Leaf Rag
Mexican Hat Dance
Sailing, Sailing
Scarborough Fair
The Star-Spangled Banner
Washington Post March
Yankee Doodle Dandy

23251 Book   US $6.95

Alfred Publishing Co., Inc.
16320 Roscoe Blvd., Suite 100
P.O. Box 10003
Van Nuys, CA 91410-0003
alfred.com

ISBN 0-7390-3775-7

0 38081 25893 5